ROCK & POP

Legends

WRITTEN BY
Ian Welch

This edition first published in the UK in 2007
By Green Umbrella Publishing

© Green Umbrella Publishing 2007

www.greenumbrella.co.uk

Publishers: Jules Gammond and Vanessa Gardner

Printed and bound in China

ISBN: 978-1-905828-71-5

The views in this book are those of the author but they are general views only and readers are urged to consult the relevant and qualified specialist
for individual advice in particular situations.

Green Umbrella Publishing hereby exclude all liability to the extent permitted by law of any errors or omissions in this book and for any loss, damage
or expense (whether direct or indirect) suffered by a third party relying on any information contained in this book.

All our best endeavours have been made to secure copyright clearance for every photograph used but in the event of any copyright owner being overlooked
please address correspondence to Green Umbrella Publishing, The Old Bakehouse, 21 The Street, Lydiard Millicent, Swindon SN5 3LU

ROCK & POP

Legends

ROCK & POP
Legends

CONTENTS

ROCK & POP *Legends*

CONTENTS

ROCK & POP *Legends*

ABBA

Line-up: Björn Ulvaeus, Benny Andersson, Agnetha Fältskog, Frida Lyngstad
First UK chart single: "Waterloo", Number 1, 1974
Trivia: Songwriters Andersson and Ulvaeus were unable to write notated music on paper

For a competition as universally derided as the Eurovision Song Contest to have introduced to the world the group who would become the biggest pop act since the Beatles is often a source of bewilderment. Yet that is what happened to Swedish superstars ABBA in 1974 when their irresistibly catchy "Waterloo" triumphed. The song was released as a single soon after and reached Number 1 in the UK and Number 6 in the States, launching a career that has seen them sell more than 370 million records worldwide (the third largest total in music history behind Elvis Presley and the Beatles).

The roots of the group dated back to 1966 when Björn Ulvaeus (born on 25 April 1945) met Benny Andersson (16 December 1946) and the pair began their musical collaboration. By the end of the 1960s, they had met the two women who were to play such a big part in their personal and professional lives. Agnetha Fältskog (born on 5 April 1950) and Anni-Frid – better known as Frida – Lyngstad (15 November 1945) were both solo recording artists in their own rights but it was as a quartet that they found international success. Ulvaeus and Fältskog were married in 1971 but it wasn't until 1978 that Andersson and Lyngstad took their own matrimonial vows.

Their first efforts were restricted to providing songs and backing vocals/instrumentation for other musicians but they found themselves on the cabaret scene in 1970 and released their first single two years later. "People Need Love" (recorded as Björn & Benny, Agnetha & Anni-Frid) was a relatively successful hit in Sweden but it gave them a taste for the stardom that was just around the corner.

The group – now called ABBA, an acronym of the initials of the members' names suggested by manager Stig Anderson – had an album's worth of material ready by the time they won the 1974 Eurovision which meant that it could be instantly released, much to the delight of the record-buying public. The album "Waterloo" reached Number 28 in the UK and was followed by 1975's "ABBA" (Number 13). This album gave them three UK hits including their second chart-topper in "Mamma Mia", a song that would later entitle a successful musical based on their unique style of music. The following year saw the release of ABBA's first "Greatest Hits" album which became their first long-player to top the UK chart.

Ironically, 1976 – the year punk was establishing itself as one of the most popular genres of music – saw ABBA enjoy huge success with the critically-acclaimed "Arrival" album. This spawned three UK chart-toppers in "Fernando", "Dancing Queen" (which

ROCK & POP *Legends*

ROCK & POP *Legends*

also provided the group's only US Number 1) and "Knowing Me, Knowing You" while the catchy "Money, Money, Money" stalled at Number 3, unable to overcome the three-week stints at the top of the charts of Chicago ("If You Leave Me Now") and Showaddywaddy ("Under The Moon Of Love").

Their subsequent offering, "ABBA – The Album", coincided with the release of "ABBA – The Movie", a feature length film about the group's 1977 Australian tour. Singles success continued with "The Name Of The Game", "Take A Chance On Me" (both UK Number 1s), "Summer Night City" (Number 5), "Chiquitita" (2) and "Does Your Mother Know" (4). By this time, however, Ulvaeus and Fältskog had announced their divorce.

As disco fever turned the music scene into one big nightclub in the late 1970s, ABBA released their sixth album "Voulez-Vous" – that gave birth to the hits "Angeleyes" (a double A-side with the title track) and "I Have A Dream" – and their second greatest hits compilation before jetting off to Australia in early 1980 for what would turn out to be their last live concerts. That year also saw the group register their final UK Number 1 singles with "The Winner Takes It All" and "Super Trouper".

Their last two studio albums – "Super Trouper" and "The Visitors" – both hit the top of the UK charts but straddled the news that Andersson and Lyngstad were also going to divorce. With Ulvaeus and Andersson concentrating on writing the musical *Chess* in 1982, the record company decided to release another compilation ("The Singles – The First Ten Years"). This proved to be an ironic choice of title as the group decided to take a break at the end of that year…one that has lasted more than 25 years! The definitive "Gold – Greatest Hits" was released in 1992 and has sold more than 26 million copies.

ABBA will forever be remembered as one of the biggest pop sensations the world has ever seen. They were also the first mainland European act to conquer both the UK and US and in November 2006 it was announced that a museum dedicated to the group was to be created in Stockholm to house costumes, instruments and other memorabilia.

LEFT
Abba performing in 1975.

BELOW
Abba with their Gold Discs for the Album "Arrival", 1976.

THE BEACHBOYS

Original line-up: Brian Wilson, Carl Wilson, Dennis Wilson, Al Jardine, Mike Love

First UK chart single: "Surfin' USA", Number 34, 1963

Trivia: The group performed initially as the Pendletones, named after the Pendleton woollen shirts popular in the 1960s

For a group whose sound epitomises the carefree joys of youth, the Beach Boys have certainly had their highs and lows over the years. The group who took vocal harmonies to new levels in the 1960s have enjoyed superstar status and chart-topping success but have also had to endure death, mental illness and legal wranglings.

Three brothers – Brian (born on 20 July 1942), Dennis (4 December 1944) and Carl Wilson (21 December 1946) – along with cousin Mike Love (15 March 1941) and friend Al Jardine (3 September 1942) began singing harmonies around the family piano in Hawthorne, California in 1961. Little did they know that this would lead them to international fame.

It was the naturally-gifted Brian who instinctively took up the creative mantle and – inspired by the vocal harmonies of the Four Freshmen – he wrote the songs and produced the recording sessions. With Carl on lead guitar and Dennis (ironically the only surfer in the group) initially on drums, the group rehearsed and eventually released their debut single "Surfin'" in December 1961. It was hardly an auspicious beginning to their career as it peaked at a lowly Number 75 in the US. The year did end on a better note, though, when the Beach Boys performed three songs at a Ritchie Valens Memorial Concert in memory of the rising star who died in the same plane crash that claimed the life of Buddy Holly on 3 February 1959.

Managed by father Murry Wilson, the Beach Boys were signed to Capitol Records the following year but by this time David Marks (born on 22 August 1948) had temporarily replaced Jardine who wanted to finish studying at college. "Surfin' Safari" was the first single to be released on the new label and this gave the Beach Boys their first US Top 20 hit but the Californian surfing revolution would not hit the UK until 1963 when "Surfin' USA" scraped into the Top 40.

It was not just the surf culture that the Beach Boys popularised but also youth and hot-rods with songs such as "Fun, Fun, Fun", "I Get Around" and "Little Deuce Coupe" but the pressure was beginning to tell on Brian and he suffered an anxiety attack in December 1964 that led to him withdrawing from touring. He was replaced for the rest of the tour by Glen Campbell and eventually Brian Johnston (born 27 June 1942).

Brian Wilson concentrated on writing new songs that contained more and more intricate harmonies and complex arrangements such as "Help Me Rhonda" and "California Girls" from 1965's "Summer Days (And Summer Nights)". But it was the

ROCK & POP *Legends*

following year's "Pet Sounds" album that defined the era...indeed, many have compared its impact to the Beatles' "Sgt Pepper" album. Paul McCartney has gone on record stating it is one of his favourite records.

The elder Wilson brother laboured in the studio for the first half of 1966, bringing in session musicians to bring his vision to fruition and only when he was satisfied were the rest of the band brought in to record the harmonies. While disappointing in commercial terms, the album does contain classics like "God Only Knows" (allegedly denied radio airplay in the States because of the word God in the title!) and "Sloop John B".

The group scored their first UK Number 1 single with "Good Vibrations", probably their best known song, taken from the 1967 album "Smiley Smile". "Good Vibrations" regularly features highly in lists of best songs of all time and is reported to have been the most expensive song ever recorded in America at the time.

Brian Wilson's health deteriorated during the late 1960s and early 1970s due to drug, weight and mental health problems and the group's output became less successful. They did score a second UK Number 1 in 1968 with "Do It Again" but after the success of "Break Away" (Number 6 in 1969) and "Cottonfields" (Number 5, 1970) it would not be until the last year of the 1970s that they again visited the UK Top 10 with "Lady Lynda".

Brian had returned to the fold in 1976 and the release of the "15 Big Ones" album was heralded as a return to form.

Tragedy struck on 28 December 1983 when Dennis – who had been suffering from alcohol and drug abuse – accidentally drowned. But the Beach Boys carried on, playing at Live Aid in July 1985 and enjoying two big hits on either side of the Atlantic. "Wipeout", with rap band the Fat Boys, was a UK Number 2 in 1987 while "Kokomo" – from the soundtrack of Tom Cruise's 1988 film *Cocktail* – gave them their first US Number 1 in 22 years.

Carl Wilson died of lung cancer on 6 February 1998 and despite Love's lawsuit against Brian Wilson over songwriting credits, the Beach Boys still tour...albeit with Love and Johnston as the only links to the past.

ROCK & POP *Legends*

THE BEATLES

Line-up: John Lennon, Paul McCartney, George Harrison, Ringo Starr
First UK chart single: "Love Me Do", Number 4, 1962
Trivia: On 25 June 1967, the Beatles became the first band ever to be globally transmitted on television to an estimated 400 million people worldwide with the specially-written "All You Need Is Love"

The world's most successful group – having sold more than one billion records – and undoubtedly the most popular, the Beatles redefined pop music in the early 1960s. Like the Beach Boys – with whom they have repeatedly been compared – the story of four lads from Liverpool is a tale of success and tragedy.

John Lennon (born on 9 October 1940), Paul McCartney (18 June 1942) and George Harrison (24 February 1943) had been playing in a local band called the Quarrymen during the late 1950s and they recruited drummer Pete Best (24 November 1941) in 1960. They perfected their sound with stints playing clubs in Hamburg and the now famous Cavern Club in Liverpool but Best was sacked by manager Brian Epstein as the group signed to EMI in 1962.

Best was replaced by Ringo Starr (born on 7 July 1940 and whose real name is Richard Starkey) and the Beatles success story was set to begin. Their debut single, "Love Me Do", was released at the end of 1962 and peaked at Number 4 in the UK charts. Beatlemania had arrived and the next eight years would see the group greeted by hordes of screaming teenage girls (and quite often their mothers!) wherever they went.

They scored their first UK Number 1 with "From Me To You" in 1963 and would go on to register another 16 chart-toppers in their career. Indeed, only "Ain't She Sweet" (1964), "Penny Lane"/"Strawberry Fields Forever" and "Magical Mystery Tour" (both 1967) spoilt a run of consecutive Number 1s that would have stretched from 1963 until 1969.

The Beatles were the first British group to have a massive impact on America. Their US record company had initially refused to release any of their first three singles but soon realised the error of their ways and the week of 4 April 1964 saw the Beatles occupy the first five slots of the Billboard Hot 100 with "Can't Buy Me Love", "Twist And Shout", "She Loves You", "I Want to Hold Your Hand" and "Please Please Me".

The four members were awarded the MBE in 1965 and two years later would record one of the most significant albums in the history of music in "Sgt Pepper's Lonely Hearts Club Band".

As often happens in successful groups though, internal tensions tore through the ranks and the Beatles played their last live gig on the top of the Apple building in London on 20 January 1969 with McCartney's lawsuit to dissolve the band in December 1970 proving the final chapter. The four members carved out solo careers after the split, with Lennon and McCartney proving the most successful.

ROCK & POP *Legends*

John Lennon had already scored a UK Number 2 with the 1969 hit "Give Peace A Chance" and 1975's "Happy Xmas (War Is Over)" equalled that placing. He registered his first chart-topper in 1975 with the classic "Imagine" and had just released his first album for five years – he had taken time out following the birth of his son Sean – when he was murdered by 'supposed' fan Mark Chapman on 8 December 1980 in New York. "(Just Like) Starting Over" and "Woman" gave him posthumous UK Number 1s but the world had lost one of its biggest talents.

Paul McCartney has been musically active ever since and registered UK Number 1s with "Mull Of Kintyre" (with Wings, 1977), "Ebony And Ivory" (with Stevie Wonder, 1982), "Pipes Of Peace" (as a solo artist, 1983) and the charity record "Ferry 'Cross The Mersey" (1989). He was knighted in 1997 but lost his wife Linda to breast cancer the following year. He married model Heather Mills in 2002 but four years later the papers were full of details of their acrimonious divorce.

George Harrison was the first to score a UK Number 1 with "My Sweet Lord" in 1971, a song that would again top the charts following his death on 29 November 2001 from lung cancer. He had also enjoyed success as one of the Traveling Wilburys with Roy Orbison, Jeff Lynne, Tom Petty and Bob Dylan. Harrison was the first rock star to organise a charity concert with 1971's Concert for Bangladesh.

Ringo Starr's post-Beatle career has been the least productive with "Back Off Boogaloo", his most successful single, peaking at Number 2 in 1972. He did score two Number 4s with 1971's "It Don't Come Easy" and You're Sixteen" (1974). He is well known to millions of children, though, as the voice behind *Thomas The Tank Engine And Friends:* Starr narrated the first two series of the television adaptation of the Rev Audrey's best-selling books.

In 1994, the three surviving members reunited to complete some unfinished John Lennon songs. "Free As A Bird" registered the highest chart position with Michael Jackson's "Earth Song" preventing a further chart-topper.

THEBEEGEES

Line-up: Barry Gibb, Maurice Gibb, Robin Gibb

First UK chart single: "New York Mining Disaster 1941", Number 12, 1967

Trivia: The Bee Gees were the first group to have UK Top 20 hits in five decades when "This Is Where I Came In" reached Number 18 in 2001

The death of Maurice Gibb on 12 January 2003 brought an end to 40 years of the Bee Gees. Although announcing their initial intention to continue, his surviving brothers Barry and Robin then decided that they would retire the group's name in memory of their sibling.

Originally hailing from the Isle of Man, Barry (born on 1 September 1946) and twins Maurice and Robin (22 December 1949) moved just outside Manchester before emigrating to Australia with their family in 1958. It was in Manchester that the trio first performed in public when a plan to lip-synch a song at a local cinema went awry after the all-important record was broken. The youngsters got on stage and sang the vocals themselves and the crowd's reaction provided all the encouragement they needed to pursue their dreams.

Within two years of heading Down Under, the trio were appearing on television shows and starting to garner a reputation for themselves and were signed to Festival Records in 1963 as the Bee Gees. The story behind the name is that the Brothers Gibb were at home with mum Barbara Gibb, a racing driver named Bill Goode and a DJ called Bill Gates who suggested that they call themselves the B Gs as there were so many people in the room with the same initials.

Although they had registered an Australian Number 1 with "Spicks And Specks" – the profits from which were used to fund their return to their native UK in January 1967 – the Bee Gees' success proved minimal until they teamed up with music industry guru Robert Stigwood and released "New York Mining Disaster 1941" which became a transatlantic Top 20 hit. They scored their first UK Number 1 later that same year with "(The Night The Lights Went Out In) Massachusetts".

The combination of Barry's lead vocals on many of the group's songs, Robin's clear vibrato (a trademark of their early music) and Maurice's high and low harmonies found an eager audience in the late 1960s and the hits continued with the UK Top 10 hits "World", "Words", "First Of May" and "Don't Forget To Remember". They also scored a second chart-topper in 1968's "I've Gotta Get A Message To You", but it was in the disco era of the mid to late 1970s that the Bee Gees really struck worldwide success.

They returned to the UK Top 5 in 1975 with the catchy "Jive Talkin'" and "You Should Be Dancing" but it was the 1977 movie Saturday Night Fever that changed the world…disco halls were soon crowded with young males wanting to be John Travolta. The

ROCK & POP *Legends*

album featuring the music became the biggest selling soundtrack of all time – more than 40 million copies were sold – and yielded the hits "How Deep Is Your Love" (Number 3), "Stayin' Alive" (4) and the chart-topping "Night Fever". These three singles were all Number 1s in the US.

The group registered their only UK Number 1 album in 1979 with "Spirits Having Flown", an impressive offering that built on the success of "Saturday Night Fever". "Too Much Heaven (UK Number 3), "Tragedy" (1), "Love You Inside Out" (13) and the title track (16) were the singles extracted from this album before the Bee Gees then decided to concentrate on other avenues. They recorded the soundtrack to the *Saturday Night Fever* follow-up *Stayin' Alive* in 1983 and worked with stars such as Barbra Streisand ("Guilty"), Diana Ross ("Chain Reaction"), Dionne Warwick ("Heartbreaker") and Dolly Parton/Kenny Rogers ("Islands In The Stream").

The Bee Gees returned to the top of the UK charts in 1987 with the upbeat "You Win Again' from the album "ESP" but the following year were mourning their younger brother. Andy – who had enjoyed a successful career as a solo artist – died just days after his 30th birthday from myocarditis, an inflammation of the heart muscle due to a viral infection.

Although the hits were not as prolific as they had previously enjoyed, the Bee Gees still registered UK Top 5 entries with "Secret Love" (1991), "For Whom The Bell Tolls" (1993), "Alone" (1997) and "Immortality" (1998). Apart from the numerous compilations, further chart albums included "Still Waters" (1997), "One Night Only" (1998) and "This Is Where I Came In" (2001)…their last studio offering before Maurice's death from a strangled intestine.

The Bee Gees may be no more, although Barry and Robin did perform together at a couple of charity concerts in 2006, but their music still lives on. Their songs are instantly recognisable and have been covered over the years by such artists as Elvis Presley, Janis Joplin, Eric Clapton, Elton John, Take That and Boyzone. The group have won seven Grammys, been inducted into the Rock'n'Roll, Songwriters and Vocal Group Halls of Fame and have received 10 Lifetime Achievement Awards.

DAVID
BOWIE

Full name: David Robert Jones

First UK chart single: "Space Oddity", Number 5, 1969

Trivia: In August 1988, Bowie portrayed Pontius Pilate in the Martin Scorsese film The Last Temptation Of Christ

W hen David Bowie celebrated his 60th birthday in 2007, radio stations played his songs every hour as a tribute, such is his enduring appeal to millions of fans. The same year also saw the 40th anniversary of his debut album, "David Bowie".

Born David Robert Jones on 8 January 1947, he changed his surname to that of Wild West hero Jim Bowie to avoid confusion with the Monkees' lead singer Davy Jones and enjoyed his first chart success with the single "Space Oddity". This release coincided with the Apollo 11 moon landing in 1969 and the story of astronaut Major Tom propelled Bowie to his first UK Top 5 hit (it would give him his first chart-topper on its re-release in 1975). The following year, Bowie married Angie Barnett and the couple celebrated the birth of their son Zowie in 1971.

Never one to stick to a particular style, Bowie had progressed from psychedelic folk to glam rock by the early 1970s (he would later embrace soul, R&B and dance) and 1972 saw the introduction of his Ziggy Stardust character on "The Rise And Fall Of Ziggy Stardust And The Spiders From Mars". This album peaked at Number 5 in the UK and spawned the single "Starman" (Number 10). He would later introduce further alter egos in Aladdin Sane and the Thin White Duke.

This success triggered the sale of his previous albums and saw "Space Oddity" (1969), "The Man Who Sold The World" (1970) and "Hunky Dory" make their chart debuts. Bowie also began producing other artists such as Mott the Hoople – for whom he wrote "All The Young Dudes', a UK Top 3 hit in 1972 – and Lou Reed.

The following year saw Bowie register his first UK Number 1 album with "Aladdin Sane" which included the Top 3 singles "The Jean Genie" and "Drive-in Saturday" and by the end of 1973 he had publicly retired Ziggy onstage at London's Hammersmith Odeon.

A chart-topping album of 1960s cover versions, "Pin Ups", preceded his next masterpiece. "Diamond Dogs", released in 1974 and also a UK Number 1, contained songs – "We Are The Dead", "1984" and "Big Brother" – from an aborted original plan to set George Orwell's iconic book *1984* to music. He enjoyed huge success in the States and further UK Top 5 albums followed through the rest of the decade with "David Live" (1974), "Young Americans" (1975), "Station To Station" and "Changesbowie" (both 1976), "Low" and "Heroes" (both 1977), "Stage" (1978) and "Lodger" (1979).

Having conquered his cocaine addiction, Bowie's second UK chart-topping single arrived in 1980 with "Ashes To Ashes" and a collaboration with Queen put him back at

ROCK & POP *Legends*

the top a year later with "Under Pressure". It was not the first time that Bowie had teamed up with another superstar; in 1977, he recorded "Peace On Earth"/"Little Drummer Boy" with Bing Crosby and this became a Yuletide Top 3 hit in 1982.

The following year saw Bowie hit mainstream success with "Let's Dance" – both the album and title single peaking at Number 1 in the UK – a change in style from his 1970s rock to embrace the now-popular dance culture that made his music much more amenable to the record-buying public. The album also spawned Top 3 singles in "Cat People (Putting Out The Fire)", "China Girl" and "Modern Love".

The follow-up, 1984's "Tonight", was seen as an attempt to cash in on the commercial success of its predecessor but contained the transatlantic Top 10 hit "Blue Jean". The 22-minute video for that song enabled Bowie to win his only Grammy to date for Best Short-Form Music Video.

The 1985 charity spectacular Live Aid provided the perfect stage for such a showman as David Bowie and he didn't disappoint. After performing classics such as "Rebel Rebel" and "Heroes", Bowie teamed up with Rolling Stone frontman Mick Jagger to strut their stuff to "Dancing In The Street". The song – a 1964 hit for Martha and the Vandellas had been written by Marvin Gaye and William "Mickey" Stevenson – enjoyed chart-topping success on its release as a single.

In 1989, he formed his first regular band in nearly 20 years in Tin Machine and three years later married Somalia-born model Iman (they have a daughter, Lexi). Bowie has continued recording and releasing new material – he registered his only UK Number 1 album of the 1990s with "Black Tie White Noise" and his only Top 10 single with "Jump They Say" (both 1993) – and has also appeared in several films.

The Albums "Heathen" (2002) and "Reality" (2003) were a welcome return to the UK Top 5 before undergoing emergency angioplasty surgery to cure a severely blocked artery that brought a period of enforced rest and a reduction in live work.

David Bowie was inducted into the Rock and Roll Hall of Fame in 1996 and was awarded a Grammy Lifetime Achievement Award 10 years later.

ROCK & POP *Legends*

THECARPENTERS

Line-up: Karen Carpenter, Richard Carpenter
First UK chart single: "(They Long To Be) Close To You", Number 6, 1970
Trivia: Karen Carpenter's only solo album was recorded in 1979 but was not released until 1996

W   ith their unique musical style, the Carpenters, from New Haven, Connecticut, were at the height of their fame during the 1970s. The style of Richard and his younger sister Karen is still adored and admired by fans today. Richard Carpenter (born 15 October 1946) was interested in music from an early age, but his sister Karen, (born 2 March) 1950 took longer to develop her musical interests.

Richard was already being influenced by Nat King Cole, Perry Como, Patti Page and Red Nichols – the legendary Dixieland jazz musician. He had a particular talent for the piano and by the age of 15 was studying at the University of Yale. When both Carpenters were in their teens, the family moved to a suburb in Los Angeles where Karen discovered that she was both interested in and had a talent for music, especially on the drums. Her supportive parents bought her a drum kit and Karen's dreams began to be realised. When Karen was just 15 years old, the Carpenter Trio was formed with school friend Wes Jacobs (a tuba and bass player). The style of the day was jazz and primarily the band were an instrumental outfit. However, Karen's voice was inspirational and Richard would urge his sister to sing. In two years her voice had begun to develop and mature and by May 1966 Karen was signed for new label Magic Lamp. Karen recorded a number of songs and two made it as singles, "Looking For Love" and "I'll Be Yours".

Despite its best efforts, the fledgling label folded within a year and the trio eventually signed to RCA but their unique sound was not enough to pull in huge amounts of money and the trio accepted a fee to opt out of their contract. Shortly after the threesome decided to disband and Jacobs headed for a career in classical music at the prestigious Juilliard.

After a brief spell in Spectrum, which suffered as a result of the increased popularity of rock bands, Richard knew a new approach was needed. However, his sister was already beginning to experience problems over her weight which would lead to her failing health at the height of their career. Karen underwent the Stillman diet (which was a barbaric regime of water and vitamins) and despite the lure of fast food – for which she had previously had a penchant – Karen stuck rigidly to the diet she hated and lost a great deal of weight. Once again, Joe Osborn (the previous owner of fated Magic Lamp) was pivotal in their career while Richard's arranging skills and Karen's singing ability were to lead the duo to greater heights.

The band were profiled on Your All American College Show and a demo tape which was heard by Herb Alpert of A&M in 1969 struck a chord. He liked their approach to

popular music amidst all the humdrum of the rock era and offered the Carpenters a deal. Their first album in 1969, "Offering" included a cover of the Beatles' "Ticket To Ride".

Burt Bacharach was also signed to A&M and he was impressed with the Carpenters' work. "(They Long To Be) Close To You" by Bacharach was the song that brought the duo critical acclaim. It led to a Number 1 single in the US charts for six weeks and won the group their first Grammy Award for Best Contemporary Vocal Performance and a further Grammy for Best New Artist, 1970. "We've Only Just Begun" became the Carpenters' signature song and, while their second album enjoyed huge success on the US chart for more than 12 months, further singles propelled Richard and Karen to stardom. However, concerns were openly expressed by Karen about her weight which had been "bulked out"

by exercise and she began a diet that she didn't need. By September 1975, it was known that Karen was suffering from anorexia nervosa and she was forced to take time out of her gruelling work schedule to recover. A year later, the Carpenters and ABC Network announced that The Carpenters Very First Television Special would be aired which was to lead to five "specials" for ABC by 1980. Their album "Made in America" was a success and, despite their own personal difficulties – Karen's eating disorder and Richard's battle to overcome his addiction to sleeping pills – the duo were back on track. Tragedy was to strike, however, on 4 February 1983 when Karen was pronounced dead of a heart attack.

The attack was an effect of her long battle against anorexia and the singer had been found unconscious at her parents' home prior to being rushed to hospital in LA. Despite Karen's untimely death, the popularity of the Carpenters has not waned and even in 1990 in the UK, the Carpenters' greatest hits compilation "Only Yesterday" became the second-biggest selling album of that year.

DURAN**DURAN**

Original line-up: Simon Le Bon, Nick Rhodes, John Taylor, Andy Taylor, Roger Taylor
First UK chart single: "Planet Earth", Number 12, 1981
Trivia: In 1984, Duran Duran was the first major act to provide giant video screens at their concerts

D uran Duran was the pop pin-up band of the early 1980s, their posters adorning the walls of millions of teenage girls around the country. Even the late Princess Diana was quoted as saying that they were her favourite band and her sons, Princes William and Harry, invited Duran Duran – along with Elton John, Brian Ferry and many others – to play at a concert held in her memory on 1 July 2007.

Duran Duran – named after a character from the 1968 sci-fi extravaganza *Barbarella* – was formed by Birmingham duo keyboardist Nick Rhodes (born Nicholas Bates on 8 June 1962) and bassist John Taylor (20 June 1960). Various other members came and went before they settled on drummer Roger Taylor (26 April 1960), guitarist Andy Taylor (16 February 1961) and vocalist Simon Le Bon (27 October 1958) in 1980 and began to work on their debut album.

Entitled "Duran Duran", it was released in 1981 and shot to Number 3 in the UK charts. The album, containing the hit singles "Planet Earth" (Number 12), "Careless Memories" (Number 37) and "Girls On Film" (Number 5), firmly established the band as part of the up and coming New Romantic scene, staying on the charts for more than two years but only becoming a bestseller in America after the re-release success of the follow-up "Rio". The video for "Girls On Film" – shot with directors Godley and Creme just two weeks after MTV was launched – proved to be extremely controversial, depicting topless girls mud wrestling and other sexual fetishes, and was banned by the BBC.

Duran Duran released their second album, "Rio" (which charted one place higher than its predecessor), in 1982 and filmed the videos to "Hungry Like The Wolf", "Rio" and "Save A Prayer" in Sri Lanka and Antigua. Unfortunately, Andy Taylor contracted malaria while the band was in these exotic locations, an event which delayed their European tour and release of their third single. These three singles all made the UK Top 10 but it was the next release that would give them their first chart-topper.

"Is There Something I Should Know?" – recorded especially for the American re-release of the band's debut album – was issued as a stand-alone single in the UK and entered the chart at Number 1 in March 1983 (just weeks after the Nick Rhodes-produced Kajagoogoo hit the top with "Too Shy"). The single would peak at Number 4 in the States.

Duran Duran released their third album "Seven And The Ragged Tiger" in December 1983. The writing and recording of the album had been an ordeal, with the band's constant partying proving a hindrance, but it gave rise to the singles "Union Of The

ROCK & POP *Legends*

Snake" (UK Number 3), "New Moon On Monday" (Number 9) and the transatlantic chart-topper "The Reflex".

Little did fans know at the time, but this would prove to be the last studio album for the current line-up for more than 20 years as their temporary break from each other became longer and longer. A live album, "Arena", was issued the following year and contained one studio recording in "The Wild Boys" which reached Number 2 on both sides of the Atlantic when released as a single.

Duran Duran also participated on the Band Aid charity record "Do They Know It's Christmas?" at the end of 1984 before recording the theme tune to the 1985 Bond film *A View To A Kill*. In 1985, the band performed at the JFK Stadium in Philadelphia for the American leg of the Live Aid charity concert but that would be the last time they played a gig together until 2003.

John and Andy Taylor formed the rock group Power Station with frontman Robert Palmer while Le Bon and Rhodes preferred to explore New Wave with Arcadia. Drummer Roger Taylor appeared in both camps.

Le Bon, Rhodes and John Taylor regrouped as Duran Duran in 1986 and released the albums "Notorious" and "Big Thing" (1989) but then suffered a succession of line-up changes. They brought in guitarist Warren Cuccurullo (born 8 December 1956) and drummer Sterling Campbell (3 May 1964) for their 1990 offering "Liberty" but Campbell had departed by 1993's "Duran Duran – The Wedding Album" which spawned a UK Number 6 hit in "Ordinary World". The same line-up also recorded "Thank You" (an album of covers in 1995) before John Taylor declared his intention to permanently leave the band in 1997.

Now a trio, Le Bon, Rhodes and Cuccurullo recorded "Medazzaland" (only released in the US, 1997) and the critically derided "Pop Trash" (2000) after which the original line-up reunited. They received the MTV Lifetime Achievement Award in 2003 and the Brit Outstanding Contribution to Music Award the following year before releasing the eagerly-awaited "Astronaut" album in October 2004. Andy Taylor again left the band two years later, as Duran Duran was working on the follow-up album.

ROCK & POP *Legends*

FLEETWOOD MAC

Most common line-up: Mick Fleetwood, Christine McVie, Lindsey Buckingham, Stevie Nicks, John McVie

First UK chart single: "Black Magic Woman", Number 37, 1968

Trivia: Only the people after whom the band was named – Mick Fleetwood and John McVie – have been ever-present

The arrival of Fleetwood Mac at the 1967 Windsor Jazz and Blues Festival heralded a career that has spanned five decades and sold more than 100 million records. Yet it was a love of blues, and not the pop/rock material for which they have since become famous, that prompted the formation of the band.

Guitarist Peter Green (born Peter Greenbaum on born 29 October 1946), drummer Mick Fleetwood (24 June 1947) and bassist John McVie (26 November 1945) were all members of John Mayall's Bluesbreakers in the 1960s but Fleetwood was sacked after getting drunk once too often. In 1967, Green decided to leave to form his own band and invited Fleetwood and McVie to join him but the latter initially declined even though his surname had been included in the band name.

With guitarist Jeremy Spencer (4 July 1948) and bassist Bob Brunning (29 June 1943) completing the initial line-up, Fleetwood Mac debuted at the Windsor Festival and, within a few weeks, McVie was convinced and replaced Brunning as the band signed to the blues label Blue Horizon Records.

This line-up recorded their eponymously-titled debut album which peaked at Number 4 in the UK charts on its 1968 release. The no-nonsense blues went down well with the record-buying public but there were unusually no singles taken from the album. As a remedy, Fleetwood Mac released "Black Magic Woman" and "Need Your Love So Bad", both UK Top 40 hits before their second album, "Mr Wonderful", hit the shelves later the same year. This featured the keyboard and vocal talents of future member (and future Mrs McVie) Christine Perfect (born on 12 July 1943), who had made her name with Chicken Shack.

Guitarist Danny Kirwan (born on 13 May 1950) had been added by the time the band's third album, "The Pious Bird Of Good Omen", only managed to hit a lowly Number 18 but it was notable for the inclusion of an instrumental song that gave them their first UK Number 1 in "Albatross". Realising that sticking with Blue Horizon would restrict their musical repertoire, the follow-up single, "Man Of The World" (a UK Number 2 hit), was released on Immediate Records and the band signed to Warner Bros.

The first album on their new label was "Then Play On", Fleetwood Mac's first rock offering, released in September 1969. A UK Number 6 hit, the American release of the album also featured the song "Oh Well" which peaked at Number 2 when released in Britain. All was not well in the Fleetwood Mac camp, however, with Green suffering from schizophrenia after having his drink spiked with LSD. His mental state was soon

questioned when he stated that he wanted to give all the band's money to charity and on 20 May 1970 he quit the group.

Mick Fleetwood took over the helm to oversee the recording of the "Kiln House" album, invited Christine McVie to join the band and – when Spencer went AWOL to join a religious sect – persuaded Green to return to help them finish their 1971 tour. But the early and mid 1970s were a torrid time for the band and the line-up changed constantly.

Their manager Clifford Davis claimed that he owned the name Fleetwood Mac and put together a rival group but the "real" Fleetwood Mac reclaimed their crown with 1975's "Fleetwood Mac" album and the critically-acclaimed 1977 chart-topping "Rumours". The line-up had now stabilised to comprise vocalist Stevie Nicks (born on 26 May 1948), guitarist Lindsey Buckingham (3 October 1949) along with Christine McVie, John McVie and Mick Fleetwood.

"Rumours" included the hit singles "Dreams", "Go Your Own Way" and "The Chain" (which later became the theme tune to the BBC's Formula 1 television programme). The band's next album, "Tusk" was released in 1979, again topping the UK charts while the 1980s saw a mix of Fleetwood Mac releases – such as 1982's "Mirage" – but the individual members also worked on their solo careers.

Fleetwood Mac regrouped for 1987's "Tango In The Night", a UK Number 1 album that included the hit singles "Little Lies" and "Everywhere" but Buckingham refused to tour the album, a decision that was to lead to a 10-year split. The remaining personnel recruited guitarists Billy Burnette (born on 8 May 1953) and Rick Vito (13 October 1949) and released the chart-topping "Behind The Mask" in 1990.

There have been various line-up changes since although Buckingham, Nicks, Fleetwood and the McVies got back together for President Clinton's Inaugural Ball in 1993 and again for a live concert in 1997 which was released as "The Dance". All five collaborated on for 2003's "Say You Will" album (UK Number 6/US Number 3) and a proposed tour is still scheduled for 2008.

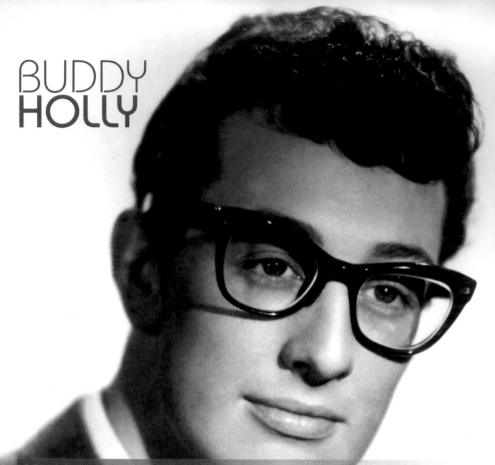

BUDDY HOLLY

Full name: Charles Hardin Holley
First UK chart single: "Peggy Sue", Number 6, 1957
Trivia: Buddy Holly is buried in Lubbock cemetery with his parents and his gravestone is engraved with a guitar

W ithout doubt, the world lost one of the greatest musical talents it had ever known when the plane carrying Buddy Holly crashed on 3 February 1959. The fact that his career lasted just a few short years but that his music still retains its enduring appeal more than half a century later gives an indication of what Holly could have achieved had he not been cut down in his prime.

Charles Hardin Holley – the change of spelling of his surname came about because of a mistake on a contract with Decca Records – was born to Laurence and Ella Holley on 7 September 1936 in Lubbock, Texas. As the youngest of the couple's four children, "Buddy", as he was known, grew up in a musical household where both his older brothers were self-taught guitarists and his sister Pat sang alongside Ella at the piano in the evenings. The family were regular church-goers in a typically segregated town, but Buddy was drawn to the "black" rhythm and blues music that filtered through to his young ears from radio stations. He began learning the piano aged 11 as well as the violin, but soon preferred the steel guitar. However, he soon picked up the acoustic guitar and the legendary singer-songwriter who was destined to achieve worldwide fame as Buddy Holly was born.

In 1951, while still at high school, Holly met Bob Montgomery. Montgomery was an accomplished guitarist and country singer who was a huge fan of Hank Williams. The pair began performing as Buddy and Bob, singing harmonies that had been influenced by their love of bluegrass music and occasionally added a bass player and drummer. The duo's fame spread and when the United States' first country radio station opened (KDAV), they were given their own weekly 30-minute programme. It was during this time that Buddy began to realise that he was a talented songwriter, although several of these compositions were not recorded until a few years later.

But it was when Buddy witnessed Elvis Presley sing live in 1955 that he realised what direction his music should be taking. This was soon confirmed when he opened for rock'n'roll legend Bill Haley and his Comets when they performed in his locality. Haley is credited as the first artist to achieve success with a rock'n'roll song when "(We're Gonna) Rock Around The Clock" became a US Number 1 in 1955 after it was used in the opening credits of the film Blackboard Jungle.

The show catapulted Holly to the big time as he was offered a solo recording contract by Decca Records. One of the first tracks he cut for Decca was the subliminal "That'll Be

ROCK & POP *Legends*

LEFT
Buddy Holly with his
band the Crickets
perform on the Ed
Sullivan show, 1957.

BELOW
Buddy Holly in
portrait, 1955.

The Day", a song whose title came from a catchphrase of John Wayne's character in the 1956 film *The Searchers*. It is probably – with "Peggy Sue" that was renamed from its original title of "Cindy Lou" – the most recognisable track that Holly would ever be associated with.

He formed a backing group called the Crickets and released an album entitled "The Chirping Crickets" in 1957 that contained tracks such as "Oh Boy!", "Not Fade Away" and a slower, higher pitched version of "That'll Be The Day" that has become synonymous with Buddy Holly. That version was recorded on 25 February 1957 and has since become a rock'n'roll staple…indeed, *Rolling Stone* magazine placed the song at number 39 in its 500 Greatest Songs of All Time.

Holly utilised a sort of hiccup in his vocal presentation that gave him a unique singing style, although Elvis did employ a similar technique. Holly married Maria Elena Santiago on 15 August 1958 and embarked on a tour of the United States with the Crickets. But his group soon became tired of life on the road and returned to Lubbock while Holly began a solo tour with other artists such as Ritchie Valens and the Big Bopper (JP Richardson).

The entourage played what would prove to be their final concert on 2 February 1959 in Clear Lake, Iowa. Holly had chartered a plane to take them to North Dakota but it crashed soon after take-off and was found a few hours later. All aboard had perished in the crash…particularly unfortunate for Valens as he had won his seat on the flight by a toss of a coin.

There have been numerous tributes paid to Buddy Holly in the intervening years. Don McLean wrote the 1971 song "American Pie" – which includes the lyric "The day the music died" – as homage to Holly, while a big fan of Buddy Holly's music, former Beatle Sir Paul McCartney, now owns the publishing rights to Holly's songs.

The tale of Holly's short life has been made into a film called The Buddy Holly Story and a stage show based around his songs still tours to sellout crowds to this day.

ROCK & POP *Legends*

MICHAEL
JACKSON

D espite all the bad publicity Michael Jackson has had to endure in recent years following his child molestation allegations, marriages, divorces and children, he was clearly born to entertain. He has reportedly sold more than 750 million albums and singles worldwide and can rightly claim to be the most successful entertainer the world has ever seen.

Jackson, born on 29 August 1958, began his singing career in 1966 with his elder brothers in the Jackson Five. (To show what a musical family the Jacksons are, sisters Janet and La Toya would also enjoy pop success.) Within two years, however, he had taken over the lead vocalist role from elder brother Jermaine and the boys had signed to Motown Records. Every one of their first four releases – "I Want You Back" (1969), "ABC", "The Love You Save" and "I'll Be There" (all 1970) – hit the top spot in the States but their only UK Number 1 was "Show You The Way To Go" in 1977. Michael remained a member of the group until 1984 and was an integral part of the disco hits "Shake Your Body (Down To The Ground)" and "Can You Feel It".

Jackson began his solo career at the tender age of 11 with the UK Top 5 singles "Got To Be There" and "Rockin' Robin". But it was with the 1979 album "Off The Wall" that the world really began to take notice. It was the first album that had ever spawned four US Top 10 hits: "Don't Stop 'Til You Get Enough" (which earned Jackson a Grammy for Best Male R&B Vocal Performance), "Off The Wall", "Rock With You" and "She's Out Of My Life". But if the sales figures of "Off The Wall" were impressive, they were about to pale into significance with his next album.

"Thriller" broke all records on its 1982 release, becoming the biggest selling album in the world with over 100 million copies sold. "Thriller" contained seven hit singles and the first to be released was a duet with Paul McCartney on "The Girl Is Mine" with its successor "Billie Jean" giving Jackson another UK Number 1. The video for this became the first by a black artist to receive regular airplay on the fledgling MTV and Jackson premiered his moonwalk while performing the song at the Motown 25: Yesterday, Today, and Forever show.

But it was the 14-minute video for the title track that stole the show. Directed by Martin Landis, the video showed Jackson being transformed into a zombie and werewolf and was the most expensive ever made at a cost of $800,000. It has since been hailed as the most popular music video of all time…indeed, such was its appeal that a documentary entitled *Making Michael Jackson's Thriller* was released that has reportedly sold 90 million copies.

It was always going to be a difficult task to live up to the success of "Thriller" – for which he had won a record seven Grammys – and the world awaited the 1987 release of "Bad" with baited breath. It was inevitable that it could not match its predecessor's sales, but "Bad" was still a commercial success with five singles – "I Just Can't Stop Loving You" (the only UK chart-topper on the album), "Bad", "The Way You Make Me Feel", "Man In The Mirror" and "Dirty Diana" – reaching the US Number 1 spot.

His next albums were "Dangerous" in 1991 – which included the controversial Number 1 "Black Or White" – and "HIStory" (1995), a two-disc package that comprised 15 greatest hits and 15 new compositions. Two of these new songs – "You Are Not Alone" and "Earth Song" – both hit the UK Number 1 spot, as did the title track of his 1997 album "Blood On The Dancefloor".

The new millennium saw the arrival of the "Invincible" album in 2001, but the days of releasing the majority of tracks as singles were long gone. "You Rock My World" was the highest charting of the two this album offered, peaking at Number 2 in the UK. "Visionary: The Video Singles" was released as a boxset in early 2006 with Jackson working on a forthcoming album due in late 2007.

But it is his personal life that Michael Jackson has made most headlines with. Whether it be his Neverland ranch with its own amusement park, or him sleeping in an oxygen tent and wearing a surgical mask whenever venturing out in public, Jackson was rarely out of the papers in the 1980s and 1990s.

His much publicised child molestation allegations coupled with controversy over his finances and the after-effects of plastic surgery have done much to harm his reputation and his marriages to and subsequent divorces from Lisa Marie Presley and Debbie Rowe (with whom he had two children, Prince Michael II and Paris) have not helped either. It remains to be seen whether Michael Jackson can rebuild his reputation and credibility to the levels he previously enjoyed.

ROCK & POP *Legends*

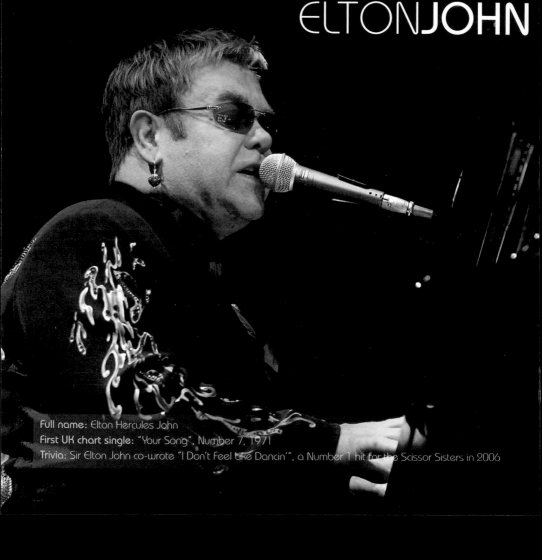

ELTON**JOHN**

Full name: Elton Hercules John
First UK chart single: "Your Song", Number 7, 1971
Trivia: Sir Elton John co-wrote "I Don't Feel Like Dancin'", a Number 1 hit for the Scissor Sisters in 2006

One of the most flamboyant entertainers there has ever been, Elton John has sold more than 250 million records and seen his career span more than five decades. The Liberace of the pop world, Elton's concerts are an instant sell-out and he has popularised the use of piano in the genre.

Born Reginald Dwight on 25 March 1947, his parents were music buffs so from a young age Elton was listening to a diverse range of piano in music with the likes of Nat King Cole, George Shearing, Rosemary Clooney and Frank Sinatra. He began playing piano at the age of three and a year later his parents were asking him to perform at parties. He discovered rock'n'roll at the age of nine and won a scholarship to the Royal Academy of Music two years later but although his classical tuition was to prove vital, his heart belonged to Ray Charles, Elvis Presley and Bill Haley.

In 1964, Elton and some friends formed a band and fellow members Elton Dean and Long John Baldry inadvertently supplied his future stage name. He supplemented any money from gigging by running errands for a music publishing company but his big break came in 1967 when he answered an advert in the New Musical Express. Ray Williams, A&R manager for Liberty Records, met Elton and gave him some lyrics written by another person who had answered the ad: Bernie Taupin. It was the start of one of the most successful partnerships in music.

The pair spent the first couple of years writing songs for others, with Elton doubling up as a session musician but it was the 1970 release of his eponymously-titled second album – the previous year's "Empty Sky" had failed to set the charts alight – that started the ball rolling. The single "Your Song", that was originally the B-side of "Take Me To The Pilot", provided Elton with his first chart hit, peaking at Number 7 in the UK and one place lower in the States.

The 1970s proved to be a very successful decade for Elton John, with hit albums such as "Tumbleweed Connection" (UK Number 2, 1971), "Honky Chateau" (Number 2, 1972), "Don't Shoot Me, I'm Only The Piano Player" and "Goodbye Yellow Brick Road" (both Number 1, 1973), "Caribou" (Number 1, 1974 and the autobiographical "Captain Fantastic And The Brown Dirt Cowboy" (Number 2, 1975). Single highlights of this period included "Rocket Man" (Number 2, 1972), "Crocodile Rock" (Number 5, 1972), "Daniel" (Number 4, 1973), "Pinball Wizard" (Number 7, 1976, from the Who's rock opera *Tommy*) and "Song For Guy" (Number 4, 1978).

ROCK & POP *Legends*

He also registered a UK Number 11 in 1974 with "Candle In The Wind", a tribute to Marilyn Monroe. Elton John would rewrite the lyrics following the death of his friend Princess Diana in 1997, changing "Goodbye Norma Jean" to "Goodbye England's Rose". He sang this version at her funeral but declared that he would never perform the song again. It was released as a single and topped the charts in almost every country, eventually going on to sell a staggering 33 million copies with the proceeds being donated to her memorial fund. Elton John was also one of the stars who were invited by her sons, Princes William and Harry, to perform at her memorial concert in July 2007.

In 1976, Elton hit the UK Number 1 slot for the first time, singing a duet with Kiki Dee on "Don't Go Breaking My Heart". It would take him until 1990 to score a solo UK chart-topper, when the double A-side "Sacrifice"/"Healing Hands" hit the peak. He would record another three solo UK Number 1s in "Sorry Seems To Be The Hardest Word" (a 2002 re-recording of his 1976 hit), "Are You Ready For Love" (2003) and "Ghetto Gospel" (with rapper 2Pac in 2005) while his duet of "Don't Let The Sun Go Down On Me" with George Michael at the Freddie Mercury Tribute Concert also provided him with a 1991 chart-topper.

The hits continued throughout the coming decades with "I'm Still Standing" (1983), "Nikita" (1985), "True Love" (1993) and "Electricity" (2005) but he also indulged in his other love: football. He became chairman of Watford Football Club in 1976 and enjoyed the thrills and spills of taking them into the First Division and to the 1984 FA Cup Final where they lost to Everton. He sold the club in 1987 but was back 10 years later and remains president. One of his other great passions is cars and his garage has housed Bentleys, Ferraris, Aston Martins and Rolls Royces.

On a personal level, Sir Elton John – he was knighted in 1998 – and his long-time partner David Furnish were one of the first gay couples to enter into a civil partnership on 21 December 2005 once the law had been changed.

LEFT
Elton at his flamboyant best in an open-air concert, 1974.

BELOW
Elton John and his long standing writing partner, Bernie Taupin.

ELTON JOHN AIDS FOUNDATION

TOMJONES

Full name: Thomas John Woodward
First UK chart single: "It's Not Unusual", Number 1, 1965
Trivia: Tom's grandson Alexander competed in the 2006 Commonwealth Games, representing Wales as a Full-Bore marksman

A sk your mother or even your granny who their favourite male solo singer is and odds are that quite a few will name Tom Jones. Often dubbed the "sex bomb", Jones was rewarded for his services to music with a knighthood in 2006.

It's a far cry from the valleys of south Wales where he was born Thomas John Woodward on 7 June 1940. The son of a miner, Tom's powerful voice soon became apparent and – despite a bout of tuberculosis that kept him in bed for nearly a year – he donned an all-leather outfit and joined local band Tommy Scott and the Senators as lead singer in 1963. They worked hard at building their reputation but nationwide acclaim was elusive and a demo made with famed producer Joe Meek failed to persuade any record labels to take a chance.

London-based manager Gordon Mills – originally from south Wales himself – saw Tom perform at the Top Hat in Cwmtillery and realised that here was a star in the making. He took him to London, renamed him Tom Jones after the 1963 film of the same name and the rest is history.

Although many record companies were not convinced, Jones signed to Decca and released his debut single "Chills And Fever" in 1964…it flopped. The follow-up, however, would set Tom Jones on a chart career that has spanned more than 40 years. The BBC refused to play "It's Not Unusual", co-written by Mills and Les Reed, until it was championed by Radio Caroline, a pirate station operating from a boat in international waters off the southeast coast of England. From then on it was just a matter of time until the song hit the top of the UK chart (it was also a US Top 10 hit) in March 1965. Further hits followed that year with "With These Hands" and "What's New Pussycat?" and Jones was awarded a Grammy for Best New Artist.

In 1966, Jones was invited to follow in the footsteps of Matt Monro and Shirley Bassey and sing the theme to the fourth James Bond film *Thunderball*. Jones reportedly fainted while recording the final note, explaining: "I closed my eyes and I held the note for so long when I opened my eyes the room was spinning".

Tom Jones then enjoyed his biggest selling single ever with a song that Jerry Lee Lewis had released earlier in 1966. "Green, Green Grass Of Home" was released in November and knocked the Beach Boys' "Good Vibrations" from the top of the UK charts, a position it held for seven weeks. Despite many misconceptions, the song is not about Wales but is an American country song about a man in a prison cell awaiting execution.

ROCK & POP *Legends*

The following year saw Jones perform in Las Vegas for the first time and he struck up a friendship with his American counterpart, Elvis Presley. Tom began spending more time playing the clubs – where women would often throw their underwear at him onstage – than recording but still enjoyed a successful spell in the charts with the Top 5 hits "I'll Never Fall In Love Again", "I'm Coming Home", the perennial favourite "Delilah", "Help Yourself", "Daughter Of Darkness" and "Till". He also recorded several hit albums including the chart-topping "Delilah", "This Is Tom Jones" and "Tom Jones Live In Las Vegas".

Despite his own television variety show in the late 1960s/early 1970s, his star faded somewhat after his "20 Greatest Hits" compilation became a UK Number 1 in 1975 and it wasn't until his son Mark took over Tom's management following the death of Mills in 1986 that his career was resurrected.

"A Boy From Nowhere" was a UK Number 2 in 1987 but it was the following year's cover of Prince's "Kiss", recorded with the Art of Noise, that really brought Tom Jones back into the public eye. He performed a medley of songs from the hit film The Full Monty at the 1998 Brit Awards ceremony with Robbie Williams and this was followed the following year by the Number 1 album "Reload" which went on to sell more than four million copies. This was a collection of duets with artists such as the Cardigans ("Burning Down The House"), Cerys Matthews ("Baby, It's Cold Outside"), the Stereophonics ("Mama Told Me Not To Come") and Mousse T ("Sex Bomb").

In 2002, he again threw his critics by recording the Top 40 album "Mr Jones" with Wyclef Jean from the Fugees and he recorded an album with Jools Holland in 2004. On 28 May 2005, Tom Jones performed in Pontypridd to celebrate his 65th birthday, his first gig there in more than 40 years, before teaming up with Chicane in April 2006 for the dance hit "Stoned In Love". He may be a pensioner, but Tom Jones shows no signs of slowing down!

LEFT
Tom Jones, with his ever faithful female fans, 1969.

BELOW
Tom collected his Knighthood in 2006.

MADONNA

Full name: Madonna Louise Ciccone

First UK chart single: "Holiday", Number 6, 1984

Trivia: With her views on President George Bush well publicised, Madonna has expressed her support for Hillary Clinton in the 2008 presidential elections

The self-styled queen of pop, Madonna can claim numerous records including the most successful female recording artist of all time, with her record label quoting sales figures in excess of 200 million. She has registered 34 consecutive UK Top 10 singles while in her native US she holds the (female) record with 27 consecutive Top 20 entries and 10 chart-toppers.

Madonna Louise Ciccone was born the third of six children on 16 August 1958 but suffered heartache early in her life when her mother died of breast cancer in 1963. Her father insisted that his children take music lessons but the young Madonna persuaded him to let her study dance…a move which paid off when she won a dance scholarship to the University of Michigan. However, she was not happy and left after her second year to move to New York to try to make her name as a dancer.

Life was hard and she was forced to take a succession of low-paid jobs including nude modelling to eke out a living. But she was learning her trade in bands such as the Breakfast Club and Emmy before she was signed to Sire Records in 1982. Her contract dictated that she would be paid $5,000 per song.

Her debut singles "Everybody" and "Burning Up"/"Physical Attraction" failed to hit the charts but the record company kept faith and her first album "Madonna" was released in 1984. This yielded the UK Top 10 singles "Holiday" and "Borderline" and set the stage for Madonna to rule the world.

The follow-up album, "Like A Virgin", topped the UK and US charts and has since gone on to sell over 17 million copies. It contained the UK Top 5 singles "Material Girl", "Crazy For You", Angel, "Dress You Up" and the title track while "Into The Groove" – from the film Desperately Seeking Susan – gave Madonna her first UK chart-topper in 1985. She enjoyed further UK Number ones in the 1980s with "Papa Don't Preach", "True Blue", "La Isla Bonita", "Who's That Girl" and "Like A Prayer".

The world's fascination with Madonna continued throughout the 1990s as – with her "Immaculate Conception" greatest hits package selling 26 million copies – just three of her 29 UK chart singles failed to reach the Top 10. She scored two more chart-toppers in "Vogue" and "Frozen" and released successful albums in "True Blue", "You Can Dance" and "Like A Prayer".

In the early 1990s, Madonna courted controversy on numerous occasions with her book *Sex* (with explicit photographs of the star taken by Steve Meisel), the *Basic Instinct*

ROCK & POP *Legends*

wannabe film, *Body Of Evidence* and videos such as "Erotica" (which MTV only showed three times due to its content) and "Justify My Love" (which featured various fetishes). But her albums – "Erotica", "Bedtime Stories" and "Something To Remember" – were never out of the UK Top 3.

She enjoyed a revitalised period of success with the critically-acclaimed 1998 album "Ray Of Light" that won her three Grammys for Best Dance Recording, Best Pop Album and Best Recording Package. She also hit the charts with "Beautiful Stranger" – recorded for the *Austin Powers, The Spy Who Shagged Me* film soundtrack in 1999 – and that garnered yet another Grammy, this time for Best Song Written for a Motion Picture, Television or Other Visual Media.

Her follow-up album "Music" was better received than its successor "American Life" but there was a return to form with 2005's "Confessions On A Dance Floor". It contained four hit singles including the UK Number ones "Hung Up" and "Sorry".

It's not just her music that Madonna is famous for, she has also appeared in several films including *Who's That Girl?*, *Dick Tracy*, *A League Of Their Own* and the 1996 adaptation of Andrew Lloyd Webber's musical *Evita* (for which she won a Golden Globe Award for Best Actress in a Musical or Comedy). She is already a published children's author and became the face of H&M in the summer of 2006 and launched her own fashion line – M by Madonna – in March 2007.

Madonna – married to third husband, film director Guy Ritchie, since December 2000 – already had two children of her own, Lourdes and Rocco, but hit the headlines in October 2006 when she adopted a baby boy from a Malawian orphanage despite the fact that his father was still alive. She even found herself on Oprah Winfrey's chat show having to defend her actions.

Madonna shows no signs of fading and, with her undoubted aptitude to reinvent herself, is still hitting the Number 1 spot regularly and winning awards. She was nominated for three Grammys including two for her "Confessions On A Dance Floor" album and during 2007 was busy working on her next release.

ROY
ORBISON

Nicknamed "The Big O", Roy Orbison was an instantly recognisable and extremely successful singer-songwriter whose career spanned four decades. His songs have been recorded by such luminaries as Buddy Holly, the Everly Brothers and Jerry Lee Lewis, and he has toured with legends like the Beach Boys and the Rolling Stones.

He was born Roy Kelton Orbison on 23 April 1936 in Vernon, Texas, but his family moved to Fort Worth during the Second World War. Interested in music at a particularly tender age, the youngster asked his father for a harmonica for his sixth birthday but was instead surprised by a guitar and so a legend was born. Roy and his brother Grady were sent to live with their maternal grandmother in Vernon due to an outbreak of polio in 1944 and it was at this time that he wrote his first composition "A Vow Of Love". He won a talent contest two years later and formed his first band, the Wink Westerners, in 1949.

The band were appearing regularly on KERB radio by the time Orbison graduated from Wink High School in 1954 before attending North Texas State College and then Odessa Junior College. The Wink Westerners were allotted their own 30-minute weekly shows on local television and one of their guests happened to be Johnny Cash. He suggested that they contact his record producer Sam Phillips but they were initially turned down. The producer famed for discovering Elvis Presley relented, however, and Roy Orbison began his career with Sun Records in Memphis.

Orbison first found success with "Ooby Dooby" in June 1956 which peaked at Number 56. The song had been written by two of his college friends but one of his own compositions soon rocketed to the top of the US charts. "Claudette" – the name of his first wife who would die in a motorcycle accident in 1966 – was offered to the Everly Brothers who backed it with their A-side "All I Have To Do Is Dream" in 1958. The death of Claudette was not the only personal tragedy Orbison had to endure: he was away on a European tour in 1968 when his Tennessee home burned to the ground, killing two of his three sons.

By 1960, Orbison was hitting the big time in his own right and "Only The Lonely" soon became one of his signature tunes. It peaked at Number 2 in the States and went one place better in the UK and signalled the arrival of Roy Orbison on the international music scene.

Further hits followed such as "Running Scared", and in 1963 he headlined a European tour with new sensations the Beatles. He became such good friends with the band that they asked him to manage their US tour (he had no choice but to decline because of his

ROCK & POP *Legends*

work schedule). He later recorded with George Harrison in the Traveling Wilburys in the 1980s.

The following year saw him release his biggest hit "Oh, Pretty Woman". The song peaked at Number 1 in the US and went on to sell more than seven million copies. It became popular all over again when it was used as the theme for the 1990 film Pretty Woman starring Julia Roberts and Richard Gere that went on to gross $463 million worldwide.

While songs such as "Penny Arcade", "Working For The Man" and "Too Soon To Know" kept Orbison in the public eye, it was when he teamed up with Emmylou Harris in 1980 for "That Lovin' You Feelin' Again" that the music industry reaffirmed his talent with a Grammy. He teamed up with George Harrison, Jeff Lynne, Bob Dylan and Tom Petty in the Traveling Wilburys in 1988 and released the song "Handle With Care" from the album "The Traveling Wilburys Vol 1".

That title suggested that further collaborations were in the pipeline but Orbison suffered a fatal heart attack on 15 December 1988... The Big O had undergone triple heart bypass surgery 10 years earlier but his death shocked the world. "You Got It", "She's A Mystery To Me" and "I Drove All Night" were all posthumous hits as his fans tried to come to terms with his sudden demise.

Roy Orbison had been inducted into the Rock and Roll Hall of Fame in January 1987 and was honoured with the Grammy Lifetime Achievement Award in 1998 while Rolling Stone magazine placed him at number 37 in their 100 Greatest Artists of All Time in 2004.

Orbison had met his second wife Barbara in 1968 and they married the following year, building a new home just one block away from where his previous residence had been. It is Barbara who today manages his estate and keeps his memory alive for the millions of fans worldwide.

THE OSMONDS

Original Line-up: Alan Osmond, Wayne Osmond, Merrill Osmond, Jay Osmond
First UK chart single: "Down By The Lazy River", Number 40, 1972
Trivia: Donny Osmond has carved out a successful theatrical career, starring in the musicals Joseph And His Technicolour Dreamcoat as well as Beauty And The Beast

The 1970s brought the phenomenon that was the Osmonds. This all-family group from Utah began as a quartet in the early 1960s and comprised Alan Ralph Osmond (born 22 June 1949), Melvin "Wayne" Osmond (28 August 1951), Merrill Davis Osmond (30 April 1953) and Jay Wesley Osmond (2 March 1955). Despite their young age, the quartet were a resounding success and the line-up changed when younger brother Donny Osmond (born 9 December 1957) and then later "Little" Jimmy Osmond (16 April 1963) joined the group. The first break for the group came at Disneyland in Florida where the brothers' performances led them to entertain audiences of The Andy Williams Show in the 1960s. They quickly established themselves as regulars on the show and it was Jimmy Osmond who stole the moment aged only three years old.

The group were spotted by an astute record company who realised that a white group along the same lines as the Jackson 5 would be a big money-spinner. They were proved right and by the early 1970s the group were recording albums – and in 1971, Donny Osmond had his own album "The Donny Osmond Album" while he was only 14 years old. Their first single "One Bad Apple" hit the Number 1 spot in the US and stayed there for a total of five weeks selling over one million copies. Between 1971 and 1973, the Osmonds made five gold albums while Donny– the heartthrob of the family – was charting his own success in parallel with his siblings with four gold albums and seven Top 10 singles.

The next member of the family to make the "big time" was the only girl in the family, sister, Olive "Marie" Osmond (born 13 October 1959). Like her brothers, Marie was an instant success, particularly in her collaborations with brother Donny. Her hit single "Paper Roses" was a country and western song that became the singer's signature tune while her duets with Donny earned the pair worldwide recognition. It led to the *Donny & Marie* show, which was dedicated to variety performances, airing on ABC Network for three years between 1976 and 1979. Meanwhile, Jimmy Osmond was finding his own success, most notably in the UK and Japan where "I'm A Long-Haired Lover From Liverpool" was the single that particularly rocketed his career.

In a career that has spanned five decades, Donny Osmond has released an enormous amount of singles and albums and is still as popular with his fans today as he was back in the 1960s and 1970s. His career took off alongside the Osmonds and as his popularity soared worldwide he became the idol for screaming fans everywhere he went. His early

ROCK & POP *Legends*

albums have led to him releasing a staggering 56 albums including collaborations with the Osmonds, releases with Marie as well as his own personal albums. Marie Osmond, meanwhile, has found an alternative career in designing and making collector dolls. While travelling the world with the Osmonds, Marie began collecting dolls – a passion she shared with her mother, Olive. In 1991, Marie began one of the most successful collectable doll companies in the world. The first doll that Marie sculpted herself was named Olive May, after her mother, and made $3 million in its first night on QVC, the electronic retailing giant. Each doll made by Marie includes the hallmark beauty spot near its left eye – just like Marie has herself. But entrepreneurial skills don't stop with Marie.

"Little" Jimmy Osmond is also an astute businessman who has produced and promoted worldwide concert tours, commercials and ice shows as well as owning and running the Osmond Family Theatre Production company which is based in Branson, Missouri. The company offers family-orientated productions, firework displays and variety shows for the cruise-liner industry globally. In 2003, the Osmonds were rewarded for their services to the entertainment industry with a star on the Hollywood Walk of Fame.

The Osmonds are a devout Christian family who hold their beliefs dear. They remain family-orientated and believe that their Christian values are what keep them together as a close-knit family and are at the core of who they are as individuals. In 2007 the original line-up of the Osmonds, except Alan who performs rarely these days due to multiple sclerosis, will celebrate their 50th anniversary in the industry. In May 2007, they released "The Plan" on-line which Wayne Osmond described as being: "...one of the most fulfilling projects I've ever been involved with..." Today the group, including Wayne, Merrill and Jay perform a variety of musical styles including pop, rock, country and western, jazz and barbershop (where it all began back in the 1960s).

Their achievements include the sale of millions of albums and numerous gold and platinum albums along with record numbers of sell-outs for their performances. They have won the People's Choice Award, the Best Vocal Group and combine their success with a massive loyal fanbase worldwide. In the same year that the original group celebrate 50 years, Jimmy Osmond will reach his own 40th anniversary in the entertainment industry.

ELVISPRESLEY

Full name: Elvis Aaron Presley

First UK chart single: "Heartbreak Hotel", Number 2, 1956

Trivia: Elvis's twin brother Garon died at birth so he used to spell his name Aron to have a connection

E lvis Presley was the King of Rock'n'Roll. He had the voice of a black R&B or gospel singer and introduced the genre to the general public. Such was his stature that the world went into shock when he died, with millions mourning, and his Graceland estate still makes millions of dollars annually, even 30 years after his death...

Born on 8 January 1935 in Tupelo, Mississippi, he soon moved with his family to Memphis, Tennessee...a place he called home. His mother bought Elvis a guitar for his 10th birthday and the world was just a few years away from a musical revolution that still reverberates today.

In 1953, the young Elvis recorded two songs as a birthday present for his mother at the local Sun Studios in Memphis. He returned the following year to record another demo and studio owner Sam Phillips recognised his potential and asked him to record further songs. Presley's debut release was entitled "That's All Right" which became a local hit. This initial success was backed up with extensive touring and gradually more and more radio stations would play his releases.

Presley – backed by guitarist Scotty Moore (born on 27 December 1931), bass player Bill Black (17 September 1926) and drummer DJ Fontana (15 March 1931) – made his first national television appearance on the Dorsey Brothers' Stage Show in January 1956. He had signed up with the Hank Snow Attractions management company, co-owned by Colonel Tom Parker, but Parker took control of Elvis's management and, having bought out his Sun Records contract, released Elvis's first single on RCA Records. "Heartbreak Hotel" became a million-seller and gave Presley a US Number 1/UK Number 2 hit. Elvis Presley had arrived on the international scene and he scored his first UK chart-topper in 1957 with "All Shook Up".

Parker recognised that he had a star on his books and set about maximising Elvis's earning potential. The same year as his debut chart entry, Parker had Presley contracted to a seven-year movie contract with the first film, *Love Me Tender*, being released at the end of 1956. With the movies all being musicals, songs from the soundtracks were released to become chart hits and it was one of these, "Jailhouse Rock", that was to provide him with his second UK Number 1.

One hindrance to Presley's career was his mandatory national service in the US Army. He joined his unit in March 1958 and was stationed in Germany but this didn't stop the Elvis bandwagon. The film *King Creole* was released to rave reviews and he scored two UK

ROCK & POP *Legends*

Number 1s with "One Night" and "A Fool Such As I" before he was honourably discharged in March 1960.

His first UK chart-topper of 1960, "It's Now Or Never", also went on to become his best-selling single with more than 1.2 million copies sold and the two follow up singles – "Are You Lonesome Tonight?" and "Wooden Heart" – also hit the top spot and became firm fan favourites.

Despite further UK Number 1 hits with the likes of "Return To Sender", "(You're The) Devil In Disguise" and "Crying In The Chapel", Presley's star faded as the 1960s drew on. He married Priscilla Beaulieu in May 1967 and their daughter Lisa Marie was born nine months later.

He made his comeback in 1968 with a televised special – the first time he had performed live since a Pearl Harbour anniversary concert in 1961 – which led to successful live appearances in Las Vegas and across the United States. (Sadly, he did not perform any live shows outside this continent.) However, his rejuvenated popularity did not bring personal happiness.

He divorced Priscilla in 1973 and became isolated and dependent on prescription drugs. He was also overeating and began piling on the pounds. In the later years of his life, he is unrecognisable from his days as the slim teenager who had taken the world by storm less than 20 years previously.

Living life to excess took its toll on Presley and, on 16 August 1977, he was found dead at his Graceland mansion. His funeral was a national spectacle and his and his mother's bodies were moved from Memphis' Forest Hill Cemetery to the meditation gardens of Graceland after an attempted theft.

He scored a posthumous UK Number 1 with "Way Down' just weeks after his demise and – with fans refusing to believe that he was dead – there have been numerous alleged sightings of Elvis Presley from all corners of the globe in the intervening years.

Elvis Presley broke so many records that they are too numerous to mention. He was the first artist to sell one billion records (apparently 20 million of those were sold the day after he died) and holds the record for the most UK Number 1s than any other artist with 21. In 2005, many of his Number 1 hits were re-released in consecutive weeks and became Top 5 hits all over again. There has truly only ever been one King…long live the King!

PRINCE

Full name: Prince Rogers Nelson
First UK chart single: "I Wanna Be Your Lover", Number 41, 1980
Trivia: In 2001, Prince became one of Jehovah's Witnesses allegedly to satisfy his mother's dying wish

The colourful pop star Prince has been described in many ways – controversial, eccentric and a perfectionist – but there is no doubting his creative talent. A workaholic, he is credited with releasing more than 1,000 songs either under his own name or through other artists, producing most of his music himself and playing most of the instruments contained therein.

Born Prince Rogers Nelson on 7 June 1958, he had a troubled start to life when his parents separated a few years after his birth and he did not get along with his new stepfather. He moved to live with his father, who bought the youngster his first guitar. Prince played in various bands during his teenage years before signing a contract with Warner Bros in 1976.

His first four albums failed to chart in the UK and it was the title track from his 1982 album "1999" that gave him his first Top 20 hit. But it was the Purple Rain film soundtrack album – with his backing band the Revolution – that brought him to worldwide attention in 1984. The first single, "When Doves Cry", gave him a UK Number 4/US Number 1 and the re-released "1999"/"Little Red Corvette" went to Number 2 the following year. The album sold more than 13 million copies while the film grossed more than $80 million in the US.

The hit singles continued with "Let's Go Crazy", "Paisley Park" and "Raspberry Beret" while Prince took a temporary break from live shows and videos. Further film roles followed in 1986's *Under The Cherry Moon* and *Graffitti Bridge* (1990) with the former supplying the UK Number 6 hit "Kiss". In 1986 he wrote the UK Number 2 hit "Manic Monday" for the Bangles and Sinead O'Connor enjoyed a Number 1 with his "Nothing Compares 2 U" four years later.

He returned in 1987 with the album "Sign 'O' The Times" which yielded hit singles in "U Got The Look" and the title track. The album was well received by fans and critics alike…more than could be said for the following year's "Lovesexy". Although it reached Number 1 in the UK, it was a commercial disappointment having replaced the hastily withdrawn "The Black Album" as manufacture started. (This cancelled album would eventually see the light of day in 1994.)

Prince had been invited to duet with Michael Jackson on the title track of his 1987 album "Bad". Unfortunately, artistic differences meant the end of the collaboration before the project was finished. Prince was back to his solo best in 1989, providing the

ROCK & POP *Legends*

soundtrack to the *Batman* movie. The album was a transatlantic chart-topper while the single "Batdance" hit the top in the States but peaked one place lower in the UK.

The year of 1991 saw Prince enjoy a transatlantic Top 3 hit with the album "Diamonds And Pearls" with his new backing band the New Power Generation before he began to confound critics and fans with his eccentricity. Having released the single "My Name Is Prince" in 1992, he also released the album "Symbol" the same year.

The following year saw him officially change his name to the symbol that did not have a pronunciation but meant the melding of male and female symbols. Hence, he became known as TAFKAP (The Artist Formerly Known As Prince) or the Artist for short. This had all come about in a dispute with his record label who had trademarked his birth name and culminated in him appearing in public with the world "SLAVE" emblazoned on his cheek.

Disillusioned with Warner Bros, Prince began releasing albums in quick succession in an effort to fulfil his contractual obligations. His 1994 offering "Come" failed to sell more than a million copies but still hit the top spot in the UK while the following year's "The Gold Experience" produced a UK chart-topper in "The Most Beautiful Girl In The World". His last Warner Bros album was 1996's "Chaos And Disorder" and this was quickly followed by "Emancipation", released on his own NPG label, which included a cover of "Betcha By Golly Wow" (a UK Number 11 hit).

LEFT
Prince on stage, 2004.

BELOW
Prince in concert at Wembley Arena, 1990.

One more studio album followed with 1998's "Newpower Soul" before he abandoned his symbol and renamed himself Prince again in 2000. After a couple of Warner Bros "best of" albums, Prince released his most critically acclaimed albums in more than a decade with "Musicology" in 2004 and "3121" (2005). He has since contributed a song to the children's animated movie *Happy Feet* (2006) and performed at the 2006 Brit Awards.

Prince was inducted in the Rock'n'Roll Hall of Fame in March 2004 and the UK Music Hall of Fame in November 2006. That month also saw him open his own nightclub in Las Vegas where he performs his own weekly shows.

ROCK & POP *Legends*

QUEEN

Original line-up: Freddie Mercury, Brian May, John Deacon, Roger Taylor
First UK chart single: "Seven Seas Of Rhye", Number 10, 1974
Trivia: Michael Jackson suggested that Queen release "Another One Bites The Dust" as a single

From video pioneers and superstars of the 1970s, Queen became the stadium rock band of the 1980s. In Freddie Mercury they had the perfect showman and they stole the show at 1985's Live Aid.

They had assembled from the remnants of late-1960s bands Smile and Sour Milk Sea and they played their first gig in June 1970 with vocalist Freddie Mercury (born Frederick Bulsara on 5 September 1946), guitarist Brian May (19 July 1947), bassist Mike Grose and drummer Roger Taylor (26 July 1949). After a succession of bass players, they settled on John Deacon (19 August 1951) and the classic line-up was complete.

Their 1973 debut album, "Queen", failed to provide them with the breakthrough they so craved but their second offering – imaginatively entitled "Queen II" – became a UK Top 5 hit the following year as the energetic "Seven Seas Of Rhye" hit the Top 10. ("Queen" would peak at Number 24 in the chart on the back of its successor's achievement.) "Killer Queen", from their third album "Sheer Heart Attack" reached Number 2 in the UK and gave them their first US hit.

But it was the following year's "A Night At The Opera" that really caught the public's attention. The most expensive album ever made at that time, it also yielded the single "Bohemian Rhapsody" which stayed at Number 1 in the UK for nine weeks. As the band were on tour, they recorded a promotional video that could be aired on *Top Of The Pops* in their absence and this is widely credited as influencing record companies to make videos for every single they release. "Bohemian Rhapsody" would also top the charts after Mercury's death when paired with the emotive "These Are The Days Of Our Lives".

Queen played a concert in Hyde Park, London in 1976 which set new attendance records with official figures declaring that 150,000 attended the event but there were allegedly nearer 200,000 spectators. The following year saw the release of the "News Of The World" album which contained the perennial favourites "We Will Rock You" and "We Are The Champions".

The 1980s kicked off with "The Game" from which "Another One Bites The Dust", "Play The Game", "Save Me" and "Crazy Little Thing Called Love" were released as singles. The latter hit Number 2 in the UK but provided the band with their first US chart-topper while the album was notable in that it was the first Queen record to feature a synthesiser.

Queen also recorded the soundtrack to the movie *Flash Gordon* before releasing their first "Greatest Hits" album in 1981. It would prove to be an amazing success story, going

on to sell more than 25 million copies. (A second greatest hits package was released in 1991 and a third in 1999.) They played a major tour of South American stadiums and the end of that year saw a collaboration with David Bowie on the UK chart-topper "Under Pressure". Hit albums continued with "Hot Space" (1982) and "The Works" (1984) and Queen enjoyed UK Top 3 success with "Radio Ga Ga" and "I Want To Break Free".

The following year began with two shows at Brazil's Rock In Rio festival, each boasting a capacity 325,000 crowd, and in July 1985 they stole the show at Live Aid. Performing several hits including "Bohemian Rhapsody", "Radio Ga Ga", "We Will Rock You", "We Are The Champions" and "Hammer To Fall", it was the perfect stage for Freddie Mercury to really get the crowd on their feet.

They released "A Kind Of Magic" in 1986 – with music from the film *Highlander* including the title track, "Friends Will Be Friends" and the haunting "Who Wants To Live Forever" – before playing what would turn out to be their last ever live shows at Wembley and Knebworth.

LEFT
Queen on stage
in the 1980s.

BELOW
Queen, with the help
of Freddie Mercury
stole the show at Live
Aid in 1985.

Their next two studio albums, "The Miracle" and "Innuendo" (both UK Number 1s), both showcased the variety that Mercury's voice could achieve but already there were rumours circulating that Freddie was suffering from AIDS. This was confirmed on 23 November 1991 with a prepared statement from his deathbed and within 24 hours he had succumbed to the disease. Fans were publicly mourning in the streets outside his house and they showed their allegiance at a Tribute Concert in April 1992 which raised almost £20 million for AIDS charities.

In 1995, the remaining members of the band released "Made In Heaven", a studio album which Freddie Mercury had recorded the vocals to before he died. They just hadn't been able to face finishing what he had started before then…

Queen have collaborated with several artists since Mercury's death, most notably touring as Queen + Paul Rodgers – albeit without the retired Deacon – in 2005 which resulted in the release of the live album "Return Of The Champions" and the promise of a new studio album.

ROCK & POP *Legends*

CLIFF
RICHARD

Full name: Harry Rodger Webb
First UK chart single: "Move It!", Number 2, 1958
Trivia: Cliff Richard had more UK Top 10 albums in the 1980s than any other artist

The most successful solo vocalist in UK history – he has not been able to make the same impact in the United States – Sir Cliff Richard has sold more than 260 million records in a career that spans six decades. He was awarded the Outstanding Contribution to British Music at the 1989 Brit Awards and was inducted into the UK Music Hall of Fame in 2004.

Born Harry Webb in India on 14 October 1940, his family moved back to Britain following India's declaration of independence in 1947. Life was not easy for the Webb family as they had to lodge with relatives until they were granted their own council house in 1951. Having been a member of the Dick Teague Skiffle Group and the Drifters (no relation to the American band of the same name), Cliff signed a solo contract with EMI in 1958.

His debut release was a cover of Bobby Helms' "Schoolboy Crush" backed with a Cliff Richard original in "Move It!" There are various stories as to why the A- and B-sides were swapped but the fact is that they were and "Move It!" shot to Number 2 in the UK singles chart. This was quickly followed up with "High Class Baby" (Number 7), "Livin' Lovin' Doll" (Number 20) and "Mean Streak" (Number 10) as Cliff – like many others at this time – styled himself on Elvis Presley.

By this time, his Drifters backing band had changed its personnel – to include Hank Marvin, Jet Harris, Tony Meehan and Bruce Welch – and its name to the Shadows, and in 1959 they were rewarded with their own EMI recording contract. A string of hits followed such as "Apache" but the Shadows continued backing Cliff on record and on tour until they split in 1968.

Cliff Richard scored his first UK Number 1 single with 1959's "Living Doll" (a song he would again take to the top of the chart in 1986 with the cast of The Young Ones television series) and "Travellin' Light" and the following year's "Please Don't Tease" and "I Love You" before he took another leaf out of Presley's book and began starring in films.

The early-1960s proved a successful period for Cliff Richard with the hit films *The Young Ones*, *Summer Holiday* and *Wonderful Life*. The title tracks from the first two soundtrack albums provided him with further UK chart-toppers and also yielded the popular singles "When The Girl In Your Arms Is The Girl In Your Heart" and "The Next Time"/"Bachelor Boy". But as groups such as the Beatles became more popular so his record sales fell, coinciding with his conversion to Christianity.

ROCK & POP *Legends*

ROCK & POP *Legends*

He registered further Number 1s with "The Minute You're Gone" (1965) and "Congratulations", his 1968 Eurovision Song Contest entry, but struggled to maintain the same level of success throughout much of the 1970s. His image and music was reinvented with the 1976 album "I'm Nearly Famous" – which included the UK Number 9/US Number 6 hit "Devil Woman" – and "Rock'n'Roll Juvenile", three years later, that included a Number 1 single in "We Don't Talk Anymore".

Cliff released a host of successful UK Top 5 albums throughout the 1980s – including "I'm No Hero", "Love Songs", "Wired For Sound" and "Always Guaranteed" – before he claimed another chart-topping single. This time it was a Christmas Number 1 in the anthemic "Mistletoe And Wine" (1988) and he would register another Yuletide peak with 1990's "Saviour's Day".

The hit albums continued during the 1990s but his singles releases were not as numerous as they had been earlier in his career. Instead, he concentrated on the musical *Heathcliff*, an adaptation of the book *Wuthering Heights* and getting used to being called Sir Cliff Richard…in 1995 he became the first rock star to be knighted.

He continued to release Yuletide singles such as "Healing Love" (1993) and "Had To Be" (1995) but had to wait until Christmas 1999 to register his third seasonal chart-topper. With the words of "The Lord's Prayer" set to the tune from "Auld Lang Syne", "The Millennium Prayer" was a fitting Number 1 as the year 2000 arrived. Further Christmas releases included "Santa's List" (a UK Number 5 in 2003) and "21st Century Christmas" (Number 2 in 2006).

Cliff Richard and the Shadows had reunited several times over the years, but the June 2004 concert at the London Palladium was billed as the Shadows' final concert. The same year saw the release of Cliff's album "Somethin' Is Goin' On" which received rave reviews but disappointingly the sales figures did not match. He returned in 2006 with "Here And Now", an album of duets with artists such as Brian May, Barry Gibb and Daniel O'Donnell, released as he started the UK leg of his European tour, proving that the eternal Bachelor Boy is still as popular as ever.

ROCK & POP *Legends*

THEROLLINGSTONES

Original line-up: Mick Jagger, Keith Richards, Brian Jones, Bill Wyman, Charlie Watts
First UK chart single: "Come On", Number 21, 1963
Trivia: Although pianist Ian Stewart was not officially a member of the Rolling Stones after he was
sacked, he was often referred to as the sixth Stone and was inducted into the UK Music Hall of Fame
in 1989

D ubbed the Greatest Rock and Roll Band in the World, the Rolling Stones are a musical institution. Often referred to as rock's dinosaurs, they are still the world's highest earning touring band and their live shows sell out almost instantly the tickets go on sale.

Having been friends at school, Mick Jagger (born on 26 July 1943) and Keith Richards (18 December 1943) formed a group called Little Boy Blue and the Blue Boys in the early 1960s. Renaming themselves the Rolling Stones after a Muddy Waters song title, Jagger (vocals) and Richards (guitar) had been joined by guitarist Brian Jones (born on 28 February 1942), bassist Bill Wyman (real name Bill Perks, 24 October 1936) and drummer Charlie Watts (2 June 1941) by the time of their debut single release for Decca Records in July 1963. Having served an eight-month residency at the Crawdaddy Club, the Stones already had a large following and "Come On", written by rock'n'roll legend Chuck Berry, took them to Number 21 in the UK charts.

Their second single was written by the Beatles partnership of Lennon and McCartney and "I Wanna Be Your Man' peaked nine places higher than its predecessor but it was a cover of Buddy Holly's "Not Fade Away" that gave them a UK Top 3 hit in early 1964. The Stones released their eponymously-titled debut album the same year, the first of many UK Number 1s in their history.

Two more covers – "It's All Over Now" and "Little Red Rooster" – provided UK chart-toppers before they secured Number 1s with their own compositions. The Jagger/Richards-penned "The Last Time", "(I Can't Get No) Satisfaction" and "Get Off My Cloud" all hit the top spot – the latter two also giving the band their first US chart-toppers – in 1965, announcing to the world that the Rolling Stones had truly arrived and they were by now concentrating on conquering America.

The seminal "Paint It Black" gave them their sixth UK Number 1 in 1966, the year before the infamous drugs bust at Keith Richards' home which resulted in him and Jagger being given custodial sentences. Granted bail after having spent one night in cells, Jagger's sentence was eventually reduced to a conditional discharge while Richards' was quashed.

Further UK chart-toppers followed with "Jumpin' Jack Flash" and "Honky Tonk Women" as single releases became fewer and far between. The Stones returned to the blues music that had initially led them to form a band for the 1968 album "Beggars Banquet" but in June the following year Jones was sacked due to his increasing reliability

ROCK & POP *Legends*

ROCK & POP *Legends*

on drugs. He turned to drink and was found dead on 3 July 1969, his body lying at the bottom of his swimming pool.

He had been replaced by Mick Taylor (born on 17 January 1949) and the Stones played a free concert for 200,000 revellers in Hyde Park just days after his death. The critically acclaimed "Let It Bleed" – featuring "Brown Sugar" – was released in December and the Stones also enjoyed UK Number 1 albums with "Get Yer Ya-Ya's Out!" (1970), "Sticky Fingers" (1971), "Exile On Main St" (1972) and "Goat's Head Soup" (1973).

With no tour since 1973, Richards indulging more in his drug habit, Jagger living the celebrity lifestyle and refusing to acknowledge Taylor's contributions on record credits, Taylor announced that he was quitting the band. He was replaced by Ron Wood (born on 1 July 1947) who was soon thrust in at the deep end as the Stones toured America.

With Richards having cleaned up his act, 1978's "Some Girls" was hailed as a return to form but "Emotional Rescue" (1980) was panned by the critics. They redeemed themselves with the following year's "Tattoo You" before hitting the States for another tour.

There was further grief when long-time friend and road manager Ian Stewart died of a heart attack on 12 December 1985 and, by the time the group received a Grammy Lifetime Achievement Award the following year, the individual members were falling out and suffering health problems.

They returned with "Steel Wheels" in 1989 and toured the album across Europe and the US, but in 1993 Wyman announced that he had had enough of life on the road and quit the band. The other members decided not to bring in a permanent replacement, but to carry on as a quartet and it was this line-up that recorded the album "Voodoo Lounge" in 1994.

Recent releases have seen the Stones enjoy UK Top 10 entries with the albums "Bridges To Babylon" (1997), the "Forty Licks" compilation (2002) and "A Bigger Bang" (2006). Richards underwent brain surgery after an alleged fall in May 2006 but was back touring with the band during 2006-07.

U2

Line-up: Bono, the Edge, Adam Clayton, Larry Mullen Jr
First UK chart single: "Fire", Number 35, 1981
Trivia: The first "U2-charist" – an adapted Holy Communion service that uses the group's best-selling songs in place of hymns – was staged in the United States in 2005

I rish rockers U2 announced their arrival in the early 1980s and have been pounding out the hits ever since. They have sold more than 120 million albums and won a record 22 Grammy awards. Not bad for a band formed in Dublin in 1976 and who – two years later – would win a St Patrick's Day talent show in Limerick. The prize was £500 and the opportunity to record a demo.

The band members – vocalist Bono (born Paul Hewson on 10 May 1960), guitarist the Edge (born Dave Evans on 8 August 1961), bassist Adam Clayton (13 March 1960) and drummer Larry Mullen Jr (31 October 1961) – have been together since day one when they were initially called Feedback and then the Hype. They eventually settled on the name U2 in 1978 and an EP called "Three" was released in Ireland in late 1979. A few months later the band played their first London gigs before another Ireland-only single ("Another Day") was released.

Signed to Island Records, U2's debut album "Boy" was released in October 1980 but it initially failed to chart in the UK. It was only after "Fire", the first single from the follow-up album "October", became a Top 40 hit the following year that "Boy" crept to Number 52. Further low-key single success followed with "Gloria" and "A Celebration" before 1983's "New Year's Day" gave them their first UK Top 10 entry. It also reached Number 53 in America, where the video was an MTV favourite that helped gain them fans across the Atlantic.

"New Year's Day" was taken from the band's third studio offering "War", their UK Number 1 album that also included the seminal "Sunday Bloody Sunday" (written about the troubles in Northern Ireland). It also contained the single "Two Hearts Beat As One", a UK Number 18 in 1983.

The same year saw U2 release their first live album in "Under A Blood Red Sky" before they scored their biggest UK hit with the Martin Luther King-inspired "Pride (In The Name Of Love)" (Number 3) the following year. "The Unforgettable Fire" – named after paintings by survivors of the Hiroshima and Nagasaki bombings – gave U2 their second UK chart-topping album before the band hit the tour treadmill once more.

With the band working on their next album – although Bono had contributed vocals to Band Aid's "Do They Know It's Christmas?" – fans had to be content with live performances and they don't come any bigger than Live Aid. In July 1985, U2 took part in the Bob Geldof-organised spectacular that has since gone down in history as the most

ROCK & POP *Legends*

influential concert ever. As would be expected from a band of their stature, U2 took it all in their stride and gained many new fans in the process. They also headlined 1986's A Conspiracy of Hope Tour for Amnesty International.

But it was the 1987 album "The Joshua Tree" that catapulted them into the major league. It was the first UK release to sell a million copies on CD and gave them a transatlantic Number 1, winning two Grammys in the process. The singles "With Or Without You" and "I Still Haven't Found What I'm Looking For" both hit Number 1 in the States (Numbers 4 and 6 respectively in the UK). They scored their first UK Number 1 single with "Desire", taken from the following year's "Rattle And Hum" album.

They continued to take between two and four years to release new studio albums and they were all transatlantic chart-toppers (apart from their first offering of the 1990s which stalled at Number 2 in the UK). Fans and critics alike lapped up "Achtung Baby" (1991), "Zooropa" (1993) and "Pop" (1997). They enjoyed UK Number 1 singles with "The Fly" (1991) and "Discotheque" (1997) and also contributed to the *Batman Forever* and *Mission: Impossible* film soundtracks.

Their first greatest hits compilations were released in 1998, along with a re-recording of a "Joshua Tree" B-side, "Sweetest Thing", whose video saw Bono apologising to his wife Alison for forgetting her birthday. As per Alison's wishes, the proceeds from the single went to the Chernobyl Children's Project International charity.

They continued their UK chart-topping success with the albums "All That You Can't Leave Behind" (2000) and "How To Dismantle An Atomic Bomb" (2004) and the singles "Beautiful Day" (2000), "Take Me To The Clouds Above", "Vertigo" (both 2004) and "Sometimes You Can't Make It On Your Own" (2005). They won five Grammys in 2006 for Album of the Year, Song of the Year, Best Rock Album, Best Rock Performance By a Duo or Group with Vocal and Best Rock Song.

They released the "U218 Singles" compilation in late 2006 which contained two new songs: "The Saints Are Coming" with American superstars Green Day and "Window In The Skies". U2 spent 2007 working on their next studio album release.

LEFT
U2 on one of their American tours.

BELOW
Lead singer of U2 Bono, in 1984.

ROBBIE
WILLIAMS

Full name: Robert Peter Williams
First UK chart single: "Freedom", Number 2, 1997
Trivia: Robbie Williams is estimated to be worth more than £100 million

Since 1997, Robbie Williams has enjoyed a hugely successful solo career following his fairly acrimonious split with former band Take That. His career has seen the flamboyant artist sell more albums than any other UK solo artist in history and sales stand at almost 50 million worldwide. Single sales are more than 15 million – with five and half million being sold in the UK alone – and he has appeared in the all-time Top 100 biggest selling albums list six times. Williams has had eight Number 1 albums and six Number 1 singles in the UK and has won many awards.

"Life Thru A Lens" was his first solo album in 1997 and included the Number 2 UK hit "Old Before I Die", "Lazy Days" (Number 8) and "Angels" which reached Number 4. Critics were waiting to see what Williams could do. But the dynamic performer proved he had the ability, talent and determination to make it big when the single "Angels" was released. Despite not making it into the Top 3, "Angels" became his biggest-selling single with 868,000 copies sold and remained in the charts for a total of 27 weeks. Riding on the back of the single's success, the album returned to the charts and went on to become Williams' first Number 1 album. A year later, his second album, "I've Been Expecting You", spent 98 weeks on the UK chart. "Millennium" was the single taken from the album which gave Williams his first Number 1 in the UK while "No Regrets" reached Number 4 while "She's The One" gave him another chart-topper.

"The Ego Has Landed" in 1999 was released exclusively in the US and all songs were taken from the first two albums. Sales in Canada reached more than 100,000 and the album went platinum. Worldwide, the album went on to sell nearly a million copies. In 2000, a fourth album, "Sing When You're Winning", featured a duet with star Kylie Minogue. The single, "Kids" went to Number 2 while "Rock DJ" and "The Road To Mandalay" gave him his next two Number 1 singles.

The following year saw the release of "Swing When You're Winning" which has a US-style big band swing and jazz sound from the 1930s and 1940s. The album – comprised entirely of covers – proves Williams' capabilities as a master of other musical genres. The duet with Nicole Kidman, "Somethin' Stupid" was another chart-topper for Williams while "Have You Met Miss Jones" was included on the film soundtrack to Bridget Jones' Diary. "Escapology" in 2002 was the final album he worked on with co-songwriter and producer Guy Chambers. The album did not receive rave reviews from some critics, but fans adored it and other critics heralded it a triumph.

ROCK & POP *Legends*

ROCK & POP *Legends*

The exciting "Live At Knebworth" the following year was sorely robbed of the Number 1 spot by Dido's "Life For Rent". A compilation of songs from his three sold-out live gigs at Knebworth – including "Angels", "Let Me Entertain You" and "She's The One" – it is an electrifying album of Williams at his best.

Nine years after starting out on a solo career, Williams released his "Greatest Hits" in 2004. Straight in at the Number 1 spot, the album was one of the fastest-selling albums in the UK and produced his sixth Number 1 single in "Radio" which had not been released on the earlier albums. A year later "Intensive Care" became a Number 1 album for Williams and the best-selling album of 2005. "Rudebox" in 2006 was the 10th album for Williams. The title track reached Number 4 in the UK chart, although it did top the charts in a number of countries worldwide and was the best-selling single in Europe for several weeks.

Williams' "Close Encounters Tour" – named after his increasing interest in the extra-terrestrial – in 2006 kicked off in Dublin at Croke Park. With support acts the Beautiful South and Basement Jaxx for the European leg of the tour, the gig at Roundhay Park in Leeds also became the first UK concert to be broadcast live in High-Definition (HD). Dates in Hong Kong, Singapore and Shanghai were cancelled, however he finished the eight-month tour in Melbourne, Australia in December to a crowd of three and a half million.

Williams set up the charity Give It Sum in June 2000 with the help of Comic Relief. Give It Sum improves local conditions across North Staffordshire where money is given to those who are disadvantaged. More than £2 million has already been given to around 126 projects in the community. In addition, Williams and his long-time friend Jonathan Wilkes organised a charity football match at Old Trafford in Manchester in 2006 where teams consisted of celebrities. The event raised more than £1 million for Africa.

ROCK & POP *Legends*

ALSO AVAILABLE IN THIS SERIES

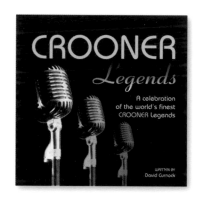

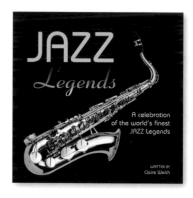

THE PICTURES IN THIS BOOK WERE PROVIDED COURTESY OF THE FOLLOWING:

GETTYIMAGES
101 Bayham Street, London NW1 0AG

PHPHOTOS
www.paphotos.com

Concept and Creative Direction:
VANESSA and KEVINGARDNER

Design and Artwork: KEVINGARDNER

Image research: ELLIECHARLESTON

PUBLISHED BY GREEN UMBRELLA PUBLISHING

Publishers:
JULESGAMMOND and VANESSAGARDNER

Written by: IANWELCH